# PRE-APPRENTICESHIP
## MATHS & LITERACY FOR
# ELECTRICAL
## graduated exercises and practice exam

Andrew Spencer

**A+ National Pre-Apprenticeship Maths & Literacy for Electrical**
**1st Edition**
**Andrew Spencer**


Associate publishing editor: Jana Raus
Project editor: Jana Raus
Senior designer: Vonda Pestana
Text design: Vonda Pestana
Cover design: Ami-Louise Sharpe
Cover image: Corbis Australia
Photo research: Libby Henry
Production controller: Alex Ross
Reprint: Jess Lovell
Typeset by Macmillan Publishing Solutions

Any URLs contained in this publication were checked for currency during the production process. Note, however, that the publisher cannot vouch for the ongoing currency of URLs.

**Acknowledgements**
We would like to thank the following for permission to reproduce copyright material:

PhotoEdit/Davis Barber: p. 38; Photolibrary: p. 32.

Every effort has been made to trace and acknowledge copyright. However, if any infringement has occurred the publishers tender their apologies and invite the copyright holders to contact them.

For product information and technology assistance,
in Australia call **1300 790 853**;
in New Zealand call **0800 449 725**

For permission to use material from this text or product, please email
**aust.permissions@cengage.com**

ISBN 978 0 17 046403 1

**Cengage Learning Australia**
Level 7, 80 Dorcas Street
South Melbourne, Victoria Australia 3205

**Cengage Learning New Zealand**
Unit 4B Rosedale Office Park
331 Rosedale Road, Albany, North Shore 0632, NZ

For learning solutions, visit **cengage.com.au**

Printed in Australia by Ligare Pty Limited.
1 2 3 4 5 6 7 25 24 23 22 21

# A+ National

# PRE-APPRENTICESHIP
## Maths & Literacy for Electrical

# Contents

# Introduction

It has always been important to understand, from a teacher's perspective, the nature of the mathematical skills students need for their future, rather than teaching them textbook mathematics. This has been a guiding principle behind the development of the content in this workbook. To teach maths that is *relevant* to students seeking apprenticeships is the best that we can do, to give students an education in the field that they would like to work in.

The content in this resource is aimed at the level that is needed for a student to have the best possibility of improving their maths and literacy skills specifically for trades. Students can use this workbook to prepare for an apprenticeship entry assessment, or to even assist with basic numeracy and literacy at the VET/TAFE level. Coupled with the NelsonNet website, https://www.nelsonnet.com.au/free-resources, these resources have the potential to improve the students' understanding of basic maths concepts that can be applied to trades. These resources have been trialled, and they work.

Commonly used trade terms are introduced so that students have a basic understanding of terminology that they will encounter in the workplace environment. Students who can complete this workbook and reach an 80 per cent or higher outcome in all topics will have achieved the goal of this resource. These students will go on to complete work experience, do a VET accredited course or be able to gain entry into VET/TAFE or an apprenticeship in the trade of their choice.

The content in this workbook is the first step to bridging the gap between what has been learnt in previous years, and what needs to be remembered and re-learnt for use in trades. Students will significantly benefit from the consolidation of the basic maths and literacy concepts.

Every school has students who want to work with their hands, and not all students want to go to university. The best students want to learn what they do not know; and if students want to learn, this book has the potential to give them a good start in life.

This resource has been specifically tailored to prepare students for sitting apprenticeship or VET/TAFE admission tests, and for giving students the basic skills they will need for a career in trade. In many ways, it is a win–win situation, with students enjoying and studying relevant maths for trades and Registered Training Organisations (RTOs) receiving students that have improved basic maths and literacy skills.

All that is needed is patience, hard work, a positive attitude, a belief in yourself that you can do it and a desire to

# About the author

achieve. The rest is up to you.

Andrew Spencer has studied education within both Australia and overseas. He has a Bachelor of Education, as well as a Masters of Science in which he specialised in teacher education. Andrew has extensive experience in teaching secondary mathematics throughout New South Wales and South Australia for well over fifteen years. He has taught a range of subject areas, including Maths, English, Science, Classics, Physical Education and Technical Studies. His sense of the importance of practical mathematics has continued to develop with the range of subject areas he has taught in.

# Acknowledgements

For Paula, Zach, Katelyn, Mum and Dad.

Many thanks to Mal Aubrey (GTA) and all training organisations for their input.

Thanks also to the De La Salle Brothers for their support and ongoing selfless work with all students. To Dr Pauline Carter also for her unwavering support of all Maths teachers.

This is for all students who value learning, who are willing to work hard and who have character . . . and are characters!

# LITERACY

## Unit 1: Spelling

### Short-answer questions

**Specific instructions to students**

- This exercise will help you to identify and correct spelling errors.
- Read the following question and then answer accordingly.

Read the following passage and identify and correct the spelling errors.

> An electrician begins work on a new two-storey construction. The toolkit includes a muldimeter, a set of plyers, renches, spaners, a set of alen keys and various screwdrivas. The apprentice turns up at 8.00 a.m. with the work vehikle. They both start work on the grownd floor. The walls need driling, so that the first set of wiares can be threeded through. The electrishan uses the 18 V drill. The battary was fully charged and did the job easerly. The apprentice goes to the work vehicle, gets the 8 m extention cord and attaches the hammar drill. He puts in a 10 mL drill bit and tightans the drill with the chuck. Four holes are driled and the main wires are put through. The ends of the wires are krimped as they finish off before having a break.

Incorrect words:

_____

_____

Correct words:

_____

_____

# Unit 2: Alphabetising

Put the following words into alphabetical order.

| | |
|---|---|
| Electrician | Fuses |
| Power surge | Crimping tool |
| Drill | Hammer drill |
| Screwdrivers | Wire |
| Multimeter | Electricity |
| Amps | Safety boots |
| Coil | Current |

_____

_____

_____

_____

_____

_____

_____

_____

_____

_____

_____

_____

_____

_____

# Unit 3: Comprehension

## Short-answer questions

### Specific instructions to students

- This is an exercise to help you understand what you read.
- Read the following passage and then answer the questions that follow.

Read the following passage and answer the questions in sentence form.

Brett the electrician started work early on Friday morning. He arrived at the building site at 5.45 a.m. Adam, who is also a 'sparky', arrived 45 minutes later. A new security system needed to be put in and Brett started unloading the work van. Adam grabbed the toolbox and checked that the multimeters were fully charged. Brett brought out the CCTV (closed circuit TV) components and both began to set up the job.

Once the ladder was in place, Brett took the cordless drill from the van, loaded up some of the equipment and began to climb the ladder. He established the position that he wanted to drill the first hole in, and then he began positioning the first components of the CCTV. Pilot holes needed to be drilled first in order to allow the larger holes to be accurately drilled. Brett had completed similar jobs like this one numerous times. Meanwhile, Adam was uncoiling the wire necessary to connect the CCTV to the main electrical system. The circuit needed to be wired through the power box and the surge arrester.

Brett found that there was no problem securing all of the components due to the pilot holes he had drilled. Adam had connected up the electrical circuit without a problem and a test showed everything was working fine. Brett and Adam had a lunch break at 12.15 p.m. for an hour, and then returned to complete the last of the work. They both finished working at 4.10 p.m.

## QUESTION 1

How many hours and minutes did Adam work for the whole day?

Answer:

## QUESTION 2

What does the acronym CCTV stand for?

Answer:

## QUESTION 4

What was Adam going to use the wire that he had uncoiled for?

Answer:

## QUESTION 5

What did Adam and Brett need to do before they began working to know that their equipment was working fine?

Answer:

# MATHEMATICS

## Unit 4: General Mathematics

### Short-answer questions

#### Specific instructions to students

- This unit will help you to improve your general mathematical skills.
- Read the following questions and answer all of them in the spaces provided.
- No calculators.
- You will need to show all working.

QUESTION 1

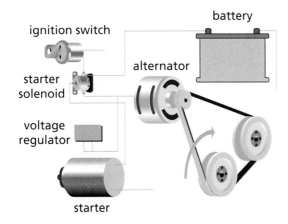

ignition switch

battery

alternator

starter solenoid

voltage regulator

starter

What unit of measurement would you use to measure:

a  electricity?

Answer:

_____

b  the resistance in an electrical circuit?

Answer:

_____

c  a length of conduit?

Answer:

_____

d  the weight of a ladder?

Answer:

_____

e  the speed of a broadband connection?

Answer:

_____

f  the frequency of a current?

Answer:

_____

g  the unit of electrical current?

Answer:

_____

QUESTION 2

Write an example of the following and give an example of where it may be found in the electrical industry.

a  percentages

Answer:

_____

b  decimals

Answer:

_____

c fractions

Answer:

_____

d mixed numbers

Answer:

_____

e ratios

Answer:

_____

f angles

Answer:

_____

## QUESTION 3
Convert the following units:

a 12 kg to grams

Answer:

_____

b 4 t to kilograms

Answer:

_____

c 120 cm to metres

Answer:

_____

d 1140 mL to litres

Answer:

_____

e 1650 g to kilograms

Answer:

_____

f 1880 kg to tonnes

Answer:

_____

g 13 m to centimetres

Answer:

_____

h 4.5 L to millilitres

Answer:

_____

## QUESTION 4
Write the following in descending order:

0.4    0.04    4.1    40.0    400.00    4.0

Answer:

_____

## QUESTION 5
Write the decimal number that is between:

a 0.2 and 0.4

Answer:

_____

b 1.8 and 1.9

Answer:

_____

c 12.4 and 12.6

Answer:

_____

d 28.3 and 28.4

Answer:

_____

e 101.5 and 101.7

Answer:

_____

## QUESTION 6

Round off the following numbers to two (2) decimal places.

a  12.346

Answer:

_____

b  2.251

Answer:

_____

c  123.897

Answer:

_____

d  688.882

Answer:

_____

e  1209.741

Answer:

_____

## QUESTION 7

Estimate the following by approximation.

a  1288 × 19 =

Answer:

_____

b  201 × 20 =

Answer:

_____

c  497 × 12.2 =

Answer:

_____

d  1008 × 10.3 =

Answer:

_____

e  399 × 22 =

Answer:

_____

f  201 − 19 =

Answer:

_____

g  502 − 61 =

Answer:

_____

h  1003 − 49 =

Answer:

_____

i  10 001 − 199 =

Answer:

_____

j  99.99 − 39.8 =

Answer:

_____

## QUESTION 8

What do the following add up to?

a  $4, $4.99 and $144.95

Answer:

_____

b  8.75, 6.9 and 12.55

Answer:

_____

c  65 mL, 18 mL and 209 mL

Answer:

_____

d  21.3 g, 119 g and 884.65 g

Answer:

_____

## QUESTION 9

Subtract the following.

a  2338 from 7117

Answer:

_____

b  1786 from 3112

Answer:

_____

c  5979 from 8014

Answer:

_____

d  11 989 from 26 221

Answer:

_____

e  108 767 from 231 111

Answer:

_____

## QUESTION 10

Use division to solve:

a  $2177 \div 7 =$

Answer:

_____

b  $4484 \div 4 =$

Answer:

_____

c  $63.9 \div 0.3 =$

Answer:

_____

d  $121.63 \div 1.2 =$

Answer:

_____

e  $466.88 \div 0.8 =$

Answer:

_____

The following information is provided for Question 11.

_____

To solve using BODMAS, in order from left to right, solve the Brackets first, then Of, then Division, then Multiplication, then Addition and lastly Subtraction. The following example has been done for your reference.

### EXAMPLE

Solve $(4 \times 7) \times 2 + 6 - 4$.

_____

**STEP 1**

Solve the Brackets first: $(4 \times 7) = 28$

**STEP 2**

No Division, so next solve Multiplication: $28 \times 2 = 56$

**STEP 3**

Addition is next: $56 + 6 = 62$

**STEP 4**

Subtraction is the last process:

_____

**FINAL ANSWER**

58

_____

## QUESTION 11

Using BODMAS, solve:

a  $(6 \times 9) \times 5 + 7 - 2 =$

Answer:

_____

b $(9 \times 8) \times 4 + 6 - 1 =$

**Answer:**

_____

c $3 \times (5 \times 7) + 11 - 8 =$

**Answer:**

_____

d $6 + 9 - 5 \times (8 \times 3) =$

**Answer:**

_____

e $9 - 7 + 6 \times 3 + (9 \times 6) =$

**Answer:**

_____

f $(4 \times 3) - 6 + 9 \times 4 + (6 \times 7) =$

**Answer:**

_____

g $(4 \times 9) - (3 \times 7) + 16 - 11 \times 2 =$

**Answer:**

_____

h $9 - 4 \times 6 + (6 \times 7) + (8 \times 9) - 23 =$

**Answer:**

_____

# Unit 5: Basic Operations

## Section A: Addition

### Short-answer questions

**Specific instructions to students**

- This section will help you to improve your addition skills for basic operations.
- Read the following questions and answer all of them in the spaces provided.
- No calculators.
- You will need to show all working.

---

#### QUESTION 1

To rewire a 2 m × 1.5 m trailer, an auto-electrician uses 2 m, 1 m, 3 m and 5 m of electrical wire. How much wire will be used in total?

Answer:

_____

#### QUESTION 2

To rewire a caravan, an auto-electrician uses 2.5 m, 1.8 m, 3.3 m and 15.2 m of electrical wire. How much electrical wire will be used in total?

Answer:

_____

#### QUESTION 3

An auto-electrical shop stocks 127 of 15 W globes, 368 of 10 W globes and 723 various globes. How many globes do they have in stock in total?

Answer:

_____

#### QUESTION 4

An electrician's van is driven 352 km, 459 km, 4872 km and then 198 km. How far has the van been driven in total?

Answer:

_____

#### QUESTION 5

An electrician uses the following amounts of diesel over a month:

Week 1: 35.5 L

Week 2: 42.9 L

Week 3: 86.9 L

Week 4: 66.2 L

a How many litres have been used in total?

Answer:

_____

b If diesel costs $1.95 per litre, how much would fuel have cost for the month?

Answer:

_____

#### QUESTION 6

If an apprentice buys a crimping tool for $22.50, 4 screwdrivers for $46.80 and a pair of pliers for $6.75, how much has been spent?

Answer:

_____

9780170464031

## QUESTION 7

An electrician uses 10 mm nuts to complete three jobs.
If he uses 26 on the first job, 52 on the second job and 48
on the third job, how many nuts have been used in total?

Answer:

## QUESTION 8

An electrician buys a new multimeter for $125.80, a
sound system for $466.99 and a subwoofer for $88.50.
How much has been spent?

Answer:

## QUESTION 9

An apprentice electrician travels 36.8 km, 98.7 km,
77.2 km and 104.3 km over four days. What distance has
he covered in total?

Answer:

## QUESTION 10

An electrician uses 178 bolts, 178 nuts and 356 washers
to complete some mechanical work on a set of power
boards. How many parts in total are needed?

Answer:

# Section B: Subtraction

## Short-answer questions

### Specific instructions to students

- This section will help you to improve your subtraction skills for basic operations.
- Read the following questions and answer all of them in the spaces provided.
- No calculators.
- You will need to show all working.

## QUESTION 1

A work vehicle is filled up to its limit of 52 L with petrol.
If the driver uses 22 L on one trip, 17 L on the second trip
and 11 L on the third trip, how much is left in the tank?

Answer:

## QUESTION 2

If an apprentice drives 362 km and another driver covers
169 km, how much further has the first driver gone?

Answer:

## QUESTION 3

P-plate driver A uses 243.8 L of LPG in a month, and
P-plate driver B uses 147.9 L of LPG in the same month.
How much more does P-plate driver A use?

Answer:

## QUESTION 4

An electrician uses 39 fuses from a box that originally
contained 163 fuses. How many fuses are left?

Answer:

## QUESTION 5

A work vehicle service costs $224.65. The mechanic takes off a discount of approximately 10%, which he then rounds off to $25.00. What does the final bill come to after the discount?

Answer:

_____

## QUESTION 6

Over a year, an apprentice drives 12 316 km. Of this, 5787 km is for his own personal use. How many kilometres did he travel for work-related purposes?

Answer:

_____

## QUESTION 7

An electrician uses the following amounts of coil for 3 jobs:

Job 1: 5.5 m

Job 2: 3.8 m

Job 3: 6.9 m

If the coil contained 50 m to begin with, how much coil is now left?

Answer:

_____

## QUESTION 8

An auto-electrician, Gary, replaces 74 globes in many different cars over a month. If there were a total of 132 globes originally, how many globes are now left?

Answer:

_____

## QUESTION 9

A car odometer has a reading of 78 769 km. An apprentice then drives some distance to work on a shack's lighting system. When she returns the car, the odometer now reads 84 231 km. How many kilometres have been travelled for the job?

Answer:

_____

## QUESTION 10

An electrical apprentice uses the following amounts of the same type of wire on 3 separate jobs: 8.7 m, 6.9 m and 15.3 m. If there were 150 m of wire to begin with, how much wire would be left?

Answer:

_____

# Section C: Multiplication

## QUESTION 1

If a car travels at 60 km/h, how far will it travel in 9 hours?

Answer:

_____

## QUESTION 2

If a car travels at 80 km/h, how far will it travel in 3 hours?

Answer:

_____

## QUESTION 3

An electrician uses 15 L of fuel for a trip to a job. How much fuel will he use if the same trip needs to be completed 26 times?

Answer:

_____

## QUESTION 4

An electrician uses 4 nuts, 8 washers and 4 bolts to secure one (1) circuit-breaker. How many nuts, washers and bolts would be used on 144 circuit-breakers?

Answer:

_____

## QUESTION 5

If 1.5 m of green wire, 2.2 m of red wire and 0.8 m of yellow wire are used on a production line for parts of the electrical system of one (1) car, how much of each wire would be used for 39 cars?

Answer:

_____

_____

## QUESTION 6

If 24 wheel nuts are used to secure four wheels on to one (1) work vehicle, how many nuts would you need for 8 vehicles?

Answer:

_____

## QUESTION 7

An electrician's vehicle uses 9 L of LPG for every 100 km she travels. How much LPG would she use to travel 450 km?

Answer:

_____

## QUESTION 8

The assembly line of an electrical company installs 673 fuses per month. If the same amount were installed each month, how many fuses would be installed over a year?

Answer:

_____

## QUESTION 9

If an auto-electrician uses 3 m of ignition coil wire each day over 28 days, how much coil has been used in total?

Answer:

## QUESTION 10

If a car travels at 110 km/h for 5 hours, how far has it travelled in total?

Answer:

# Section D: Division

## Short-answer questions

### Specific instructions to students

- This section will help you to improve your division skills for basic operations.
- Read the following questions and answer all of them in the spaces provided.
- No calculators.
- You will need to show all working.

## QUESTION 1

An auto-electrician has 24 m of cable. How many jobs can be completed if each standard job requires 3 m of cable?

Answer:

## QUESTION 2

If an electrician earns $868 for working a 5-day week, how much does she earn per day?

Answer:

## QUESTION 3

An electrical company buys 1400 m of cable in bulk. Each roll of cable contains 180 m.

a How many full rolls are there?

Answer:

b Are any rolls left over?

Answer:

## QUESTION 4

A contract electrician covers 780 km in a 5-day week. On average, how many kilometres per day have been travelled?

Answer:

## QUESTION 5

The total weight of a work van is 2488 kg. How much load, in kilograms, is on each of the 4 wheels?

Answer:

## QUESTION 6

An electrical contractor covers 1925 km over a 7-day period. How many kilometres are covered, on average, each day?

Answer:

9780170464031

## QUESTION 7

At a yearly stocktake, an apprentice electrician counts 648 fuses. If there are 12 fuses to be put into each box, how many boxes will be needed?

**Answer:**

_____

## QUESTION 8

An auto-electrician orders 408 light globes. If there are 24 globes in each box, how many boxes are there?

**Answer:**

_____

## QUESTION 9

An assembly line produces 680 power boards. The power boards will be used at 34 different locations. How many will be allocated to each location?

**Answer:**

_____

## QUESTION 10

An apprentice has 560 resistors. Of these, 28 are used on one job. How many identical jobs can be completed in total?

**Answer:**

_____

## Section A: Addition

### QUESTION 1

A set of 4 capacitors are purchased for $46.88 and a pair of pliers for $4.75. How much will be paid in total?

Answer:

### QUESTION 2

An auto-electrician buys a multimeter for $39.95, electrical wire and fittings for $29.95, several halogen light bulbs for $44.55 and some large clamps for $19.45. How much has been spent in total?

Answer:

### QUESTION 3

One length of conduit measures 9.85 m. Another length measures 12.75 m. If they need to be joined together, what will be the total length?

Answer:

### QUESTION 4

Two lengths of 50 mm conduit are to be joined together. The first length measures 100.25 cm, while the second measures 88.48 cm.

a What is the total length?

Answer:

b If they were both cut from the one original length measuring 2 m, how much is left over?

Answer:

### QUESTION 5

An electrician buys the following: a tool belt for $38.99, a fan belt for $6.50, 200 staples for $12.30 and a single gang box for $65.90. What is the total cost?

Answer:

### QUESTION 6

If a contract electrician travels 65.8 km, 36.5 km, 22.7 km and 89.9 km over 4 days, how far has he travelled in total?

Answer:

## QUESTION 7

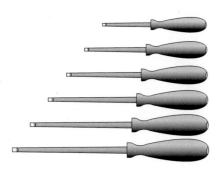

What is the total length of a screwdriver with an insulated handle of 11.5 cm and a shaft of 7.8 cm?

Answer:

_____

## QUESTION 8

A light switch has a height of 2.42 cm. If the height of the backing is 3.5 cm, what is the total height of the switch and backing?

Answer:

_____

## QUESTION 9

An auto-electrician completes three jobs. He charges $450.80 for the first job, $1130.65 for the second job and $660.45 for the third job. How much has he charged in total for all three jobs?

Answer:

_____

## QUESTION 10

An apprentice needs to seal around the edge of a circuit board that is 18.8 cm long by 9.85 cm wide. What is the total length around the perimeter?

Answer:

_____

# Section B: Subtraction

## Short-answer questions

### Specific instructions to students

- This section will help you to improve your subtraction skills when working with decimals.
- Read the following questions and answer all of them in the spaces provided.
- No calculators.
- You will need to show all working.

## QUESTION 1

An electrician trims a wire on a board. If the wire measures 38 cm and 9.95 cm is cut off, what length will be left?

Answer:

_____

## QUESTION 2

If an electrician cuts off 22.5 cm from a cable that is 1.5 m long, how much is left?

Answer:

_____

## QUESTION 3

An apprentice electrician completes a job that costs $789.20 and then a discount of $75.50 is given. How much is the final cost?

Answer:

_____

## QUESTION 4

An apprentice 'sparky' works 38 hours and earns $245.60. On pay day, he spends a total of $48.85 on petrol, oil and food. How much is left?

Answer:

_____

## QUESTION 5

An auto-electrician needs to get to some wiring under a car. The car-jack is raised to a height of 65.6 cm. It is then lowered by 8.95 cm to get to the wiring. What height is it now at?

Answer:

_____

## QUESTION 6

If a length of conduit that electrical wire is passed through has a diameter of 9.5 cm and a different length has a diameter of 8.85 cm, what is the difference between the two diameters?

Answer:

_____

## QUESTION 7

The distance between each of 4 resistors in a series is 32.50 mm. The distance between 2 other resistors is 31.85 mm. What is the difference in distance?

Answer:

_____

## QUESTION 8

An electrician has a 6 m length of copper pipe. He uses the length for 3 different jobs: 2.85 m for job 1, 0.56 m for job 2 and 1.3 m for job 3.

a  How much is needed for all 3 jobs?

Answer:

_____

b  How much is left over?

Answer:

_____

## QUESTION 9

An auto-electrician has 2 lengths of 10 m cable. He uses 350 cm on one job, 765 cm on another job, and then a further 445 cm on the final job.

a  How much cable is used overall?

Answer:

_____

b  How much cable is left?

Answer:

_____

## QUESTION 10

A set of speakers needs to be re-wired. If the apprentice has 6 m of wire and uses 257 cm, how much is left?

Answer:

_____

9780170464031

# Section C: Multiplication

## QUESTION 1

If one tyre on an electrician's van costs $99.95 and he needs to purchase a total of 5 tyres (4 for each wheel and 1 for the spare), how much will the total cost be?

Answer:

## QUESTION 2

If an electrician uses 1 m of copper pipe that costs $20.50 per metre, what is the cost of 15 m?

Answer:

## QUESTION 3

An apprentice electrician replaces 6 fluorescent lights at a cost of $4.50 each. She then replaces 8 fuses at a cost of $3.99 per fuse. What is the total cost of the lights and the fuses?

Answer:

## QUESTION 4

If an apprentice purchases 6 packets of 10 mm nuts that cost $8.65 per packet, how much is the total cost?

Answer:

## QUESTION 5

An auto-electrician buys 12 packets of 15 W fuses that cost $9.95 each. How much did he spend in total?

Answer:

## QUESTION 6

An electrician's hourly rate is $33.50. How much will she earn for a 45-hour week?

Answer:

## QUESTION 7

An electrical workshop owner purchases 25 m of air-conditioning hose. The cost of the hose is $2.55 per metre. How much did he spend in total?

Answer:

## QUESTION 8

A contractor fills up their 52 L car petrol tank at $1.55 per litre. How much does the contractor pay for the petrol?

Answer:

_____

## QUESTION 9

An electrical company purchases 340 gang boxes. The cost of each box is $30.15. What is the outlay?

Answer:

_____

## QUESTION 10

An apprentice electrician earns $80.65 per day. How much is his gross pay for a 5-day week?

Answer:

_____

# Section D: Division

## Short-answer questions

### Specific instructions to students

- This section will help you to improve your division skills when working with decimals.
- Read the following questions and answer all of them in the spaces provided.
- No calculators.
- You will need to show all working.

## QUESTION 1

An electrician needs to evenly allocate 288 fuses (each fuse is 15 W) for 6 separate jobs. How many are needed for each job?

Answer:

_____

## QUESTION 2

An electrician earns $1590.60 for 5 days of work. How much does she earn per day?

Answer:

_____

## QUESTION 3

An electrical contractor travels 525 km over 3 days. How far does he travel, on average, each day?

Answer:

_____

## QUESTION 4

An auto-electrician completes a job worth $440.85. If the job takes 16 hours to complete, what is the hourly rate?

Answer:

_____

 9780170464031

## QUESTION 5

A semitrailer driver drives from Adelaide to Darwin with electrical supplies. He covers 2568 km over 5 days. How far has he travelled, on average, each day?

**Answer:**

_____

## QUESTION 6

An apprentice electrician drives from Adelaide to Melbourne for a trade expo. She travels a total of 889.95 km over 11 hours. What distance did she travel, on average, each hour?

**Answer:**

_____

## QUESTION 7

A work vehicle uses 36 L to travel 288.8 km. How far does the car travel per litre?

**Answer:**

_____

## QUESTION 8

An electrician orders 360 spark plugs at a cost $1890 for a workshop. How much is the cost of one spark plug?

**Answer:**

_____

## QUESTION 9

It costs $80.95 to fill a work van's 52 L fuel tank. How much is the cost per litre?

**Answer:**

_____

## QUESTION 10

A 50 m roll of heater hose costs $83.60. How much does the hose cost per metre?

**Answer:**

_____

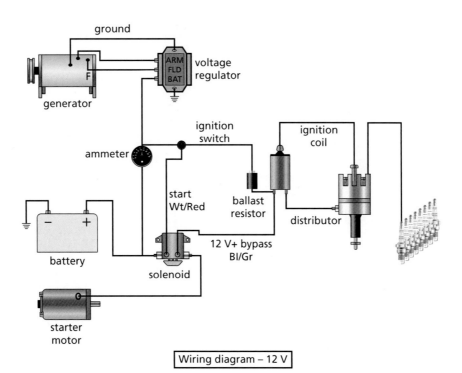

Wiring diagram – 12 V

# Unit 7: Fractions

## Section A: Addition

**QUESTION 1**

$\frac{1}{2} + \frac{4}{5} =$

Answer:

_____

**QUESTION 2**

$2\frac{2}{4} + 1\frac{2}{3} =$

Answer:

_____

**QUESTION 3**

A bolt is inserted $\frac{2}{4}$ of the way through a wall. If it is pushed another $\frac{1}{5}$ through, how far has the bolt been pushed through the wall? Express your answer as a fraction.

Answer:

_____

**QUESTION 4**

A gang nail is hammered $\frac{1}{3}$ of the way into a gyprock wall. It is then hammered a further $\frac{2}{5}$ into the wall. How far has it gone into the wall? Express your answer as a fraction.

Answer:

_____

**QUESTION 5**

An aerial connecting wire is fed $\frac{3}{4}$ of the way through a hole in a wall. If it is then fed a further $\frac{1}{6}$ in, how far has the aerial been fed through the wall in total? Express your answer as a fraction.

Answer:

_____

## Section B: Subtraction

## QUESTION 1

$\frac{2}{3} - \frac{1}{4} =$

**Answer:**

_____

## QUESTION 2

$2\frac{2}{3} - 1\frac{1}{4} =$

**Answer:**

_____

## QUESTION 3

An electrician has $2\frac{2}{3}$ rolls of cable. $1\frac{1}{2}$ are used on a housing job. How much cable now remains? Express your answer as a fraction.

**Answer:**

_____

## QUESTION 4

An apprentice has $5\frac{1}{2}$ packets of screws. If $3\frac{1}{3}$ packets are used on a repair job, how many boxes are left? Express your answer as a fraction.

**Answer:**

_____

## QUESTION 5

An electrician takes $2\frac{1}{2}$ rolls of coil to an industrial complex for use on a repair job. The electrician uses $1\frac{1}{3}$ of the rolls to complete the job. How much coil is left? Express your answer as a fraction.

**Answer:**

_____

# Section C: Multiplication

## QUESTION 1

$\frac{2}{4} \times \frac{2}{3} =$

**Answer:**

_____

## QUESTION 2

$2\frac{2}{3} \times 1\frac{1}{2} =$

**Answer:**

## QUESTION 3

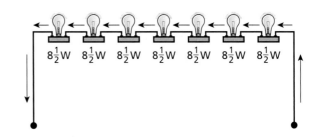

$8\frac{1}{2}$W  $8\frac{1}{2}$W  $8\frac{1}{2}$W  $8\frac{1}{2}$W  $8\frac{1}{2}$W  $8\frac{1}{2}$W  $8\frac{1}{2}$W

Seven lights are connected in series. If each light uses $8\frac{1}{2}$ W, how many watts are there in total? Express your answer as a fraction.

**Answer:**

_____

## QUESTION 4

A battery weighs $1\frac{1}{2}$ kg. How much will 12 batteries weigh?

Answer:

_____

## QUESTION 5

A wiring job requires 6 lengths of red wire that each measure $18\frac{1}{2}$ cm, 8 lengths of green wire that each measure $16\frac{1}{2}$ cm, and 4 lengths of yellow wire that each measure $20\frac{1}{2}$ cm. How much of the red, green and yellow wire is needed to complete the job?

Answer:

_____

_____

# Section D: Division

## QUESTION 1

$\frac{2}{3} \div \frac{1}{4} =$

Answer:

_____

## QUESTION 2

$2\frac{3}{4} \div 1\frac{1}{3} =$

Answer:

_____

## QUESTION 3

An apprentice has a 50 m roll of electrical cable. It needs to be cut into $6\frac{1}{2}$ m lengths.

a How many lengths can be cut?

Answer:

_____

b Is there any wastage?

Answer:

_____

## QUESTION 4

An electrician needs to cut $3\frac{1}{2}$ cm machine bolt blanks from a 2 m length of steel stock. How many bolt blanks can be cut?

Answer:

_____

## QUESTION 5

An auto-electrician has $6\frac{1}{2}$ packets of screws that are to be used on 4 separate jobs. How many packets will be needed for each job? Express your answer as a fraction.

Answer:

_____

# Unit 8: Percentages

10% rule: Move the decimal one place to the left to get 10%.

**Example**

10% of $45.00 would be $4.50.

## QUESTION 1

An electrical repair bill comes to $1220.00. How much is 10% of the bill?

Answer:

_____

## QUESTION 2

A wireless reversing camera is installed at a cost of $549.00 for parts and labour.

a What is 10% of the cost?

Answer:

_____

b If this comes off the price, what will the final cost be?

Answer:

_____

## QUESTION 3

The owner of an electrical workshop buys a 2 hp direct drive air compressor for $198.50.

a If he was given a 10% discount, how much would it work out to be?

Answer:

_____

b What would the cost of the air compressor be after the discount?

Answer:

_____

## QUESTION 4

An apprentice wants to purchase 5 rolls of solenoid coil for a total of $124.80. She is given a 5% discount by the shop owner. How much will the apprentice need to pay after the discount? (Hint: Find 10%, halve it and then subtract it from $124.80.)

Answer:

_____

## QUESTION 5

A trade assistant buys 3 storage bins for $42, an 18 V drill for $280 and a set of allen keys for $16.

a How much is the total?

Answer:

_____

b How much is paid after a 10% discount?

Answer:

_____

## QUESTION 6

The following items are purchased for a workshop: a halogen work light for $39.50; a crimping toolkit for $9.75; an air horn for $19.50; a digital multimeter for $12.30; a set of truck rear tail lights for $49.00; and a 25 m lead for $14.40.

a What is the total cost of all of the items?

Answer:

_____

b What is the final cost after a 10% discount?

Answer:

_____


## QUESTION 7

An electrical store offers 20% off the price of sets of screwdrivers. If a set is priced at $136 before the discount, how much will they cost after the discount?

Answer:

_____


## QUESTION 8

Washing machine pulley belts are discounted by 15%. If the regular retail price is $16 each, what is the discounted price?

Answer:

_____


## QUESTION 9

The regular retail price of a set of industrial drill bits costs $186.80. The store then has a 20% off sale. How much will the drill bits cost during the sale?

Answer:

_____


## QUESTION 10

A 1200 amp jump-starter retails for $99. How much will it cost after the store takes off 30%?

Answer:

_____

# Unit 9: Voltage, Current and Resistance

## Short-answer questions

### Specific instructions to students

- In this unit, you will be able to practise and improve your skills in calculating voltage, current and resistance.
- Read the following questions and answer all of them in the spaces provided.
- No calculators.
- You will need to show all working.

Ohm's law: $V = I \times R$

where:

$V$ = voltage, with volts (V) as the unit of measurement

$I$ = current, with amperes (A) as the unit of measurement

$R$ = resistance, with ohms ($\Omega$) as the unit of measurement

Transposing this formula gives the following variations:

$$I = \frac{V}{R}$$

$$R = \frac{V}{I}$$

---

### QUESTION 1

What is the voltage ($V$) of a small appliance if the current ($I$) is 12 A and the resistance ($R$) is 10 $\Omega$?

Answer:

---

### QUESTION 2

What is the resistance ($R$) if the current ($I$) is 15 A and the voltage ($V$) is 240 V?

Answer:

---

### QUESTION 3

Find the current ($I$) if the voltage ($V$) is 240 V and the resistance ($R$) is 20 $\Omega$.

Answer:

---

### QUESTION 4

Find the voltage ($V$) if the resistance ($R$) is 25 $\Omega$ and the current ($I$) is 5 A.

Answer:

---

### QUESTION 5

What is the resistance ($R$) if the current ($I$) is 25 A and the voltage ($V$) is 240 V?

Answer:

---

### QUESTION 6

Find the current ($I$) if the voltage ($V$) is 240 V and the resistance ($R$) is 50 $\Omega$.

Answer:

---

## QUESTION 7

Find the voltage (V) if the resistance (R) is 35 Ω and the current (I) is 4 A.

Answer:

## QUESTION 8

What is the resistance (R) if the current (I) is 15 A and the voltage (V) is 24 V?

Answer:

## QUESTION 9

Find the current (I) if the voltage (V) is 12 V and the resistance (R) is 0.5 Ω.

Answer:

## QUESTION 10

Find the voltage (V) if the resistance (R) is 1.5 Ω and the current (I) is 3 A.

Answer:

For Questions 11–15, note that the total resistance equals the sum of the resistors in series.

## QUESTION 11

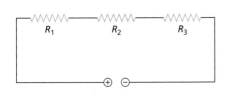

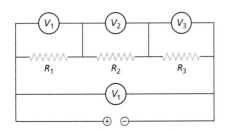

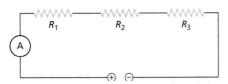

Find the total resistance ($R_t$) if resistor 1 ($R_1$) equals 130 Ω, resistor 2 ($R_2$) equals 100 Ω and resistor 3 ($R_3$) equals 180 Ω.

Answer:

## QUESTION 12

Find the total resistance ($R_t$) if $R_1$ equals 60 Ω, $R_2$ equals 110 Ω and $R_3$ equals 100 Ω.

Answer:

## QUESTION 13

Find the total resistance ($R_t$) if $R_1$ equals 0.03 Ω, $R_2$ equals 1.70 Ω and $R_3$ equals 11.0 Ω.

Answer:

## QUESTION 14

Find the total resistance ($R_t$) if $R_1$ equals 4.25 Ω, $R_2$ equals 7.5 Ω and $R_3$ equals 13.7 Ω.

Answer:

## QUESTION 15

Find the total resistance ($R_t$) if $R_1$ equals 0.5 Ω, $R_2$ equals 2.5 Ω and $R_3$ equals 3.5 Ω.

Answer:

# Unit 10: Measurement Conversions

## Short-answer questions

### Specific instructions to students

- This unit is designed to help you both to improve your skills and to increase your speed in converting one measurement unit into another.
- Read the following questions and answer all of them in the spaces provided.
- No calculators.
- You will need to show all working.

**QUESTION 1**

How many millimetres are there in 1 cm?

Answer:

_____

**QUESTION 2**

How many millimetres are there in 1 m?

Answer:

_____

**QUESTION 3**

How many centimetres are there in 1 m?

Answer:

_____

**QUESTION 4**

If a screw has 20 threads in 2 cm of its length, how many threads would there be in 10 cm?

Answer:

_____

**QUESTION 5**

How many millilitres are there in 4.8 L of de-greaser?

Answer:

_____

**QUESTION 6**

How many litres does 3500 mL of bearing grease make up?

Answer:

_____

**QUESTION 7**

A small car body weighs ½ a tonne. How many kilograms is that?

Answer:

_____

**QUESTION 8**

A ute weighs 2 t. How many kilograms is that?

Answer:

_____

**QUESTION 9**

A truck weighs 4750 kg. How many tonnes is that?

Answer:

_____

**QUESTION 10**

The wall of a shed that will have wiring running around its perimeter measures 180 cm in length and 120 cm in width. How far is it around the perimeter of the wall?

Answer:

_____

## Section A: Circumference

### Short-answer questions

**Specific instructions to students**

- This section is designed to help you both to improve your skills and to increase your speed in measuring the circumference of a round object.
- Read the following questions and answer all of them in the spaces provided.
- No calculators.
- You will need to show all working.

$C = \pi \times d$
where: $C$ = circumference, $\pi$ = 3.14 and $d$ = diameter

### EXAMPLE

Find the circumference of a plate with a diameter of 30 cm.

$C = \pi \times d$

Therefore, $C = 3.14 \times 30$

$= 94.2$ cm

### QUESTION 1

Find the circumference of a warehouse light fitting with a diameter of 60 cm.

Answer:

### QUESTION 2

Calculate the circumference of a pulley with a diameter of 15 cm.

Answer:

### QUESTION 3

Determine the circumference of a store light fitting with a diameter of 32 cm.

Answer:

### QUESTION 4

Find the circumference of a conduit with a diameter of 5 cm.

Answer:

### QUESTION 5

Calculate the circumference of a heat pump pipe with a diameter of 12 cm.

Answer:

### QUESTION 6

Determine the circumference of a spotlight fitting with a diameter of 28.8 cm.

Answer:

### QUESTION 7

Find the circumference of a car speaker hole with a diameter of 15.6 cm.

Answer:

## QUESTION 8

Determine the circumference of a 1200 W sander with a diameter of 14.3 cm.

Answer:

_____

## QUESTION 9

Find the circumference of an industrial pulley with a diameter of 42.9 cm.

Answer:

_____

## QUESTION 10

Calculate the circumference of a 50 W flood light with a diameter of 18.8 cm.

Answer:

_____

# Section B: Diameter

## Short-answer questions

### Specific instructions to students

- This section is designed to help you both to improve your skills and to increase your speed in measuring the diameter of a round object.
- Read the following questions and answer all of them in the spaces provided.
- No calculators.
- You will need to show all working.

---

$$\text{Diameter (D) of a circle} = \frac{\text{circumference}}{\pi(3.14)}$$

### EXAMPLE

Find the diameter of a conduit with a circumference of 80 cm.

$D = \frac{80}{3.14} = 25.47$ cm

## QUESTION 1

Find the diameter of a conduit with a circumference of 22 cm.

Answer:

_____

## QUESTION 2

Calculate the diameter of a ceiling hole for a light with a circumference of 16 cm.

Answer:

_____

## QUESTION 3

Determine the diameter of a CCTV camera head with a circumference of 20 cm.

Answer:

_____

## QUESTION 4

Find the diameter of a 600 W subwoofer with a circumference of 130 cm.

Answer:

_____

## QUESTION 5

Calculate the diameter of a floodlight with a circumference of 50 cm.

Answer:

_____

## QUESTION 6

Determine the diameter of a fuel tank with a circumference 11.8 m.

Answer:

_____

## QUESTION 7

Find the diameter of a conduit with a circumference of 12.4 cm.

Answer:

_____

## QUESTION 8

Calculate the diameter of a warehouse light fitting with a circumference of 90.8 cm.

Answer:

_____

## QUESTION 9

Determine the diameter of a cog with a circumference of 62.3 cm.

Answer:

_____

## QUESTION 10

Find the diameter of a storeroom light fitting with a circumference of 68.8 cm.

Answer:

_____

# Section C: Area

## Short-answer questions

### Specific instructions to students

- This section is designed to help you both to improve your skills and to increase your speed in measuring surface area.
- Read the following questions and answer all of them in the spaces provided.
- No calculators.
- You will need to show all working.

> **Area = length × breadth and is given in square units**
> $= l \times b$

## QUESTION 1

The length of an auto-electrician's trailer is 1.8 m by 1.2 m wide. What is the total floor area?

Answer:

_____

## QUESTION 2

If an electrical workshop measures 60 m by 13 m, what is the total area?

Answer:

_____

## QUESTION 3

A light switch cover is 12.8 cm by 10.6 cm. What is its total area?

Answer:

_____

## QUESTION 4

If a switchboard measures is 4.5 m by 3.8 m, what is its total area?

Answer:

_____

## QUESTION 5

If a tail light assembly plate for a trailer measures 12 cm by 10 cm, what is the total area?

Answer:

_____

## QUESTION 6

A battery has plates inside of it that measure 15.5 cm by 12.8 cm. What is the total area of one plate?

Answer:

_____

## QUESTION 7

The dimensions of the floor of an electrician's ute are 1.06 m by 1.07 m. What is the total area?

Answer:

_____

## QUESTION 8

An electrical warehouse storage area is 65.3 m by 32.7 m. How much floor area is there?

Answer:

_____

## QUESTION 9

If the floor of a garage is 3.2 m wide by 8.6 m long, what is its area?

Answer:

_____

## QUESTION 10

An electrical spare parts delivery truck is 8.9 m long and 2.6 m wide. How much floor area can it accommodate?

Answer:

_____

# Unit 12: Earning Wages

## Short-answer questions

### Specific instructions to students

- This unit will help you to calculate both how much a job is worth and how long you need to complete the job.
- Read the following questions and answer all of them in the spaces provided.
- No calculators.
- You will need to show all working.

### QUESTION 1

A first-year apprentice electrician may earn $270.45 clear per week. Based on this weekly salary, how much would the apprentice electrician earn per year? (Note that there are 52 weeks per year.)

Answer:

### QUESTION 2

An apprentice 'sparky' starts work at 8.00 a.m. and stops for a break at 10.30 a.m. for ½ an hour. He goes back to work and steadily continues until 1.15 p.m. when he stops for a lunch break for ¾ of an hour. After lunch he works through to 4.00 p.m. How many hours has he worked?

Answer:

### QUESTION 3

A trade assistant earns $15.50 an hour and works a 38-hour week. How much is her gross earnings (before tax)?

Answer:

### QUESTION 4

Over a week, an electrician completes 5 jobs, which are billed as: $465.80, $2490.50, $556.20, $1560.70 and $990.60. What do his total bills come to?

Answer:

### QUESTION 5

An apprentice auto-electrician needs to complete the following tasks:

- task 1: to remove the front panel of a car and take out some wiring, which takes 34 minutes to complete
- task 2: to remove a set of wires, which takes 18 minutes
- task 3: to replace two headlights, which takes 27 minutes
- task 4: to take out the dashboard, which takes 44 minutes
- task 5: to disconnect the speedo (speedometer), which takes 9 minutes

How much time, in total, is needed to complete all of these tasks? State your answer in hours and minutes.

Answer:

### QUESTION 6

The front room of a house needs to be rewired. This takes the electrician 4½ hours. If the pay rate is $38.50 an hour, how much will the electrician earn?

Answer:

## QUESTION 7

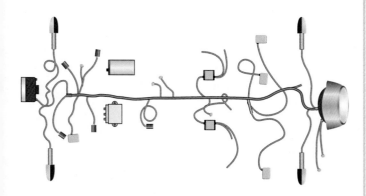

A rewiring job takes 1½ hours to complete. If the apprentice is getting paid $14.80 per hour, what amount will he earn for this job?

Answer:

_____

## QUESTION 8

A shed has electrical damage due to storms. It takes the electrician 116 hours of work to return it to a safe and workable condition. If the electrician works 8-hour days, how many days did it take?

Answer:

_____

## QUESTION 9

An apprentice begins work at 7.00 a.m. and works until 3.30 p.m. The morning break is 20 minutes, the lunch break is 60 minutes and the afternoon break is 20 minutes.

a  How much time has been spent on breaks?

Answer:

_____

b  How much time has been spent working?

Answer:

_____

## QUESTION 10

A major electrical job costs $2850.50 to complete. The apprentice spends 100 hours on the job. How much is the rate per hour?

Answer:

_____

# Unit 13: Squaring Numbers

## Section A: Introducing square numbers

**Short-answer questions**

**Specific instructions to students**

- This section is designed to help you both to improve your skills and to increase your speed in squaring numbers.
- Read the following questions and answer all of them in the spaces provided.
- No calculators.
- You will need to show all working.

---

**Any number squared is multiplied by itself.**

**EXAMPLE**

4 squared $= 4^2 = 4 \times 4 = 16$

**QUESTION 1**

$6^2 =$

Answer:

---

**QUESTION 2**

$8^2 =$

Answer:

---

**QUESTION 3**

$12^2 =$

Answer:

---

**QUESTION 4**

$3^2 =$

Answer:

---

**QUESTION 5**

$7^2 =$

Answer:

---

**QUESTION 6**

$11^2 =$

Answer:

---

**QUESTION 7**

$10^2 =$

Answer:

---

**QUESTION 8**

$9^2 =$

Answer:

---

**QUESTION 9**

$2^2 =$

Answer:

---

$4^2 =$

Answer:

_____

$5^2 =$

Answer:

_____

# Section B: Applying square numbers to the trade

## Worded practical problems

### Specific instructions to students

- This section is designed to help you both to improve your skills and to increase your speed in calculating the area of rectangular or square objects. The worded questions make the content relevant to everyday situations.
- No calculators.
- You will need to show all working.

### QUESTION 1

An apprentice sets aside a work area to work on a switchboard. The area measures 2.8 m × 2.8 m. What floor area does it take up?

Answer:

_____

### QUESTION 2

A workshop has a welding area that is 5.2 m × 5.2 m. What is the total floor area?

Answer:

_____

### QUESTION 3

The dimensions of an electrical workshop are 12.6 m × 12.6 m. What is the total floor area?

Answer:

_____

### QUESTION 4

An electrician works in an area where some rewiring is needed. The floor area is 15 m × 15 m. If the area allocated for the storage of electrical tools measures 2.4 m × 2.4 m and does not require rewiring, how much area is left to rewire?

Answer:

_____

### QUESTION 5

An auto-electrician has a total work area of 13.8 m × 13.8 m. If the spare parts area takes up 1.2 m × 1.2 m and the tool area is 2.7 m × 2.7 m, how much area is left to work in?

Answer:

_____

### QUESTION 6

An apprentice needs to construct a switchboard from material that measures 2.4 m × 2.4 m. If 1.65 m × 1.65 m is cut out initially, how much is left?

Answer:

_____

## QUESTION 7

An auto-electrician cuts out a backboard 0.5 m × 0.5 m from a sheet that is 1.2 m × 1.2 m. How much is left?

**Answer:**

_____

## QUESTION 8

A concrete work floor of an electrical workshop measures 28.2 m × 28.2 m. If it costs $9.50 to coat 1 m², how much will it cost to coat the whole floor?

**Answer:**

_____

_____

## QUESTION 9

Each wall of a welding area measures 2.6 m × 2.6 m. To insulate 1 m², it costs $28.50. How much will it cost to insulate all four walls?

**Answer:**

_____

_____

## QUESTION 10

The perimeter of a room needs to be wired. The wall measures 3.2 m × 3.2 m.

a How much wire is required to go around the outside of 3 sides of the wall?

**Answer:**

_____

b If 3 different wires need to be placed around the wall, what is the total amount of wire required?

**Answer:**

_____

## Section A: Introducing ratios

**Short-answer questions**

**Specific instructions to students**

- This section is designed to help to improve your skills in calculating and simplifying ratios.
- Read the following questions and answer all of them in the spaces provided.
- No calculators.
- You will need to show all working.
- Reduce the ratios to the simplest or lowest form.

**QUESTION 1**

The number of teeth on gear cog 1 is 40. The number of teeth on gear cog 2 is 20. What is the ratio of gear cog 1 to gear cog 2?

Answer:

**QUESTION 2**

Pulley A has a diameter of 60 cm and pulley B has a diameter of 15 cm. What is the ratio of diameter A to B?

Answer:

**QUESTION 3**

Pulley belt A has a diameter of 48 cm and pulley belt B has a diameter of 16 cm. What is the ratio of diameters of A to B?

Answer:

**QUESTION 4**

Two gear cogs have 75 and 15 teeth respectively. What is the ratio?

Answer:

**QUESTION 5**

Three cogs have 80 : 60 : 20 teeth respectively. What is the ratio?

Answer:

**QUESTION 6**

A lathe has 2 pulleys that have diameters of 16 cm and 20 cm respectively. What is the lowest ratio?

Answer:

**QUESTION 7**

The diameter of pulley A on a band saw is 32 cm. Pulley B has a diameter of 16 cm and pulley C has a diameter of 48 cm. What is the lowest ratio of the three compared together?

Answer:

**QUESTION 8**

Three pulleys have different diameters: 18 cm, 16 cm and 10 cm respectively. What is the comparative ratio?

Answer:

## QUESTION 9

Pulley A has a diameter of 34 cm and pulley B has a diameter of 12 cm. What is the ratio?

Answer:

_____

## QUESTION 10

The circumference of pulley A is 62 cm and the circumference of pulley B is 38 cm. What is the ratio?

Answer:

_____

# Section B: Applying ratios to the trade

## Short-answer questions

### Specific instructions to students

- This section is designed to help to improve your practical skills when working with ratios.
- Read the following questions and answer all of them in the spaces provided.
- No calculators.
- You will need to show all working.

## QUESTION 1

The ratio of the teeth on cog 1 to cog 2 is 3 : 1. If cog 2 has 10 teeth, how many teeth will cog 1 have?

Answer:

_____

## QUESTION 2

The ratio of the teeth on cog 1 to cog 2 is 2 : 1. If cog 2 has 20 teeth, how many teeth will cog 1 have?

Answer:

_____

## QUESTION 3

The ratio of the diameter of pulley A to pulley B is 4 : 2. If pulley A has a diameter of 40 cm, what will be the diameter of pulley B?

Answer:

_____

## QUESTION 4

The ratio of the diameter of pulley A to pulley B is 2 : 1. If pulley A has a diameter of 30 cm, what will be the diameter of pulley B?

Answer:

_____

## QUESTION 5

The ratio of teeth on cog A to cog B is 3 : 1. If the number of teeth on cog A is 12, how many teeth will be on cog B?

Answer:

_____

9780170464031

The ratio of teeth on cog A to cog B is 2 : 1. If the number of teeth on cog A is 18, how many teeth will be on cog B?

**Answer:**

---

The ratio of teeth on cog A to cog B is 3 : 1. If the number of teeth on cog A is 21, how many teeth will there be on cog B?

**Answer:**

---

The ratio of teeth on cog A to cog B is 3 : 2. If the number of teeth on cog A is 6, how many teeth will be on cog B?

**Answer:**

---

The ratio of teeth on cog A to cog B is 4 : 3. If the number of teeth on cog A is 16, how many teeth will be on cog B?

**Answer:**

---

The ratio of teeth on cog A to cog B is 4 : 3. If the number of teeth on cog A is 24, how many teeth will be on cog B?

**Answer:**

---

# Unit 15: Mechanical Reasoning

## Short-answer questions

### Specific instructions to students

- This section is designed to help to improve your skills in mechanical reasoning.
- Read the following questions and answer all of them in the spaces provided.
- No calculators.
- You will need to show all working.

## QUESTION 1

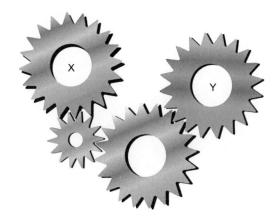

If cog X turns in a clockwise direction, which way will cog Y turn?

**Answer:**

_____

## QUESTION 2

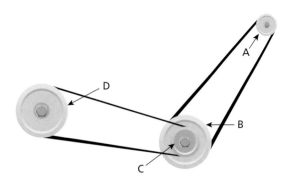

If pulley A turns in a clockwise direction, which way will pulley D turn?

**Answer:**

_____

## QUESTION 3

If the drive pulley in the following diagram of a work van engine turns in a clockwise direction, in which direction will the alternator turn?

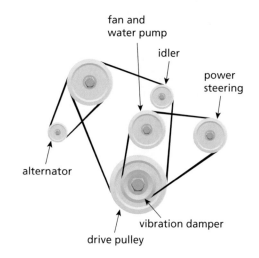

**Answer:**

_____

## QUESTION 4

Looking at the following diagram, if lever A moves to the left, in which direction will lever B move?

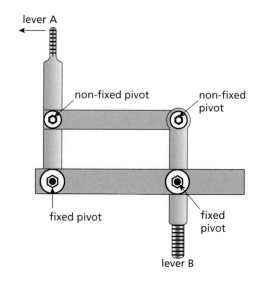

**Answer:**

_____

In the following diagram, pully 1 turns clockwise. In what direction will pully 6 turn?

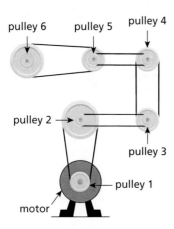

Answer:

_____

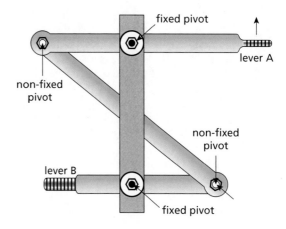

If lever A is pulled up, what will happen to lever B?

Answer:

_____

# Electrical
## Practice Written Exam for the Electrical Trade

Reading time: 10 minutes
Writing time: 1 hour 30 minutes

Section A: Literacy
Section B: General Mathematics
Section C: Trade Mathematics

## QUESTION and ANSWER BOOK

| Section | Topic | Number of questions | Marks |
|---|---|---|---|
| A | Literacy | 7 | 22 |
| B | General Mathematics | 11 | 24 |
| C | Trade Mathematics | 40 | 54 |
| | | Total 58 | Total 100 |

The sections may be completed in the order of your choice.
NO CALCULATORS are to be used during the exam.

## Spelling

10 marks

Read the passage below and then underline the 20 spelling errors.

A workshop has twulve benches for aprentices to work on. Each apprentise has his or her own toolkit that they had to perchase when they started at the company. Six of the apprentices turned up late on the first day as they could not find the workshop with the addres they were given. The company had moved premices and did not let the new workers know where their new adress was. This caused some confussion initialy, but the apprentices were smart enoufh to ring their supervisor to chek.

Once all of the apprentices had arived, got changed and were at their benches, they were all given diferent tasks to complete. One apprentice had to change five ressistors that were in serieas. Another had to replase three capasitors and several of the others needed to re-soldur circuit boards. One apprentice had to go to the storerom to retreve the soldering irons before they could begin.

Correct the spelling errors by writing them out with the correct spelling below.

_____

_____

## Alphabetising

Put the following words into alphabetical order.

7 marks

| | |
|---|---|
| Current | Circuit-breaker |
| Voltage | Capacitor |
| Power | Resistor |
| Resistance | Fuse wire |
| Ohms | Multimeter |
| Amperes | Cells |
| Wiring | Volts |

_____

_____

_____

_____

_____

_____

_____

_____

_____

_____

_____

_____

_____

_____

_____

# Comprehension

## Short-answer questions

### Specific instructions to students

* Read the following passage and then answer the questions that follow.

The VET lecturer came into class and started writing on the whiteboard immediately. It was the first lesson with this class and he wanted to introduce the students to the topics of current, voltage, power and resistance. He began with current, and explained that an electric current is the flow of electric charge. He said that the unit for measuring the sizes of electrical currents is the ampere, but everyone in the trade referred to them as 'amps'. Most of the students found this interesting, especially because of its high relevance to their chosen trade. The lecturer also pointed out that the common 8 amp or 15 amp fuses will burn out or melt if they are exposed to currents greater than these amounts.

The lecturer then moved on to the topic of voltage. He explained that electrical pressure supplied by the cell moves an electric charge through a circuit. This is known as voltage. The unit for measuring voltage is the volt. Normally, a car would use a 12 V battery and a house would use around 240 V. When the concept of power was introduced, he explained that this was the rate at which electrical appliances used electrical energy. Power is always measured in watts. He gave an example of a 60 W light bulb being brighter than a 25 W bulb. The reason for this is that a 60 W bulb uses more energy than a 25 W bulb. Some of the energy-efficient bulbs are only 8 W, and despite only using one-sixth of the power, they nevertheless give off similar brightness to a 50 W bulb.

The last topic that the lecturer introduced was resistance. He explained that the rate that electricity flows through a circuit is determined by how much resistance there is. He gave a good example of how a 60 W light bulb filament has a lower resistance than a 25 W light bulb filament. More current can then flow through the 60 W globe, thus making a brighter light. The unit that measures resistance is the ohm. The lecturer finished off by drawing some symbols and circuits that included these concepts.

## QUESTION 1                                      1 mark

What were the four topics that the lecturer introduced?

Answer:

_____

_____

## QUESTION 2                                      1 mark

In what order did he introduce the topics?

Answer:

_____

_____

## QUESTION 3                                      1 mark

What is the unit of measurement for each topic?

Answer:

_____

_____

## QUESTION 4                                      1 mark

What happens to fuses if they have too much current flowing through them?

Answer:

_____

_____

## QUESTION 5                                      1 mark

Why is a 60 W bulb brighter than a 25 W globe? How much less power does an energy-efficient globe use?

Answer:

_____

_____

_____

# Section B: General Mathematics

## QUESTION 1                                      3 marks

What unit of measurement would you use to measure:

a   current?

Answer:

_____

b   resistance?

Answer:

_____

c   voltage?

Answer:

_____

## QUESTION 2                                      3 marks

Write an example of the following and give an instance of where it may be found in the electrical industry.

a   percentages

Answer:

_____

b   decimals

Answer:

_____

c   fractions

Answer:

_____

_____

## QUESTION 3                                      2 marks

Convert the following units.

a   3 W to kilowatts

Answer:

_____

b   5 kW to watts

Answer:

_____

## QUESTION 4                                     2 marks

Write the following in descending order:

    0.7   0.71   7.1   70.1   701.00   7.0

Answer:

_____

## QUESTION 5                                     2 marks

Write the decimal number that is between:

a   0.1 and 0.2

Answer:

_____

b   1.3 and 1.4

Answer:

_____

## QUESTION 6                                     2 marks

Round off the following numbers to two (2) decimal places.

a   5.177

Answer:

_____

b   12.655

Answer:

_____

## QUESTION 7                                     2 marks

Estimate the following by approximation.

a   101 × 81

Answer:

_____

b   399 × 21

Answer:

_____

## QUESTION 8                                     2 marks

What do the following add up to?

a   $7, $13.57 and $163.99

Answer:

_____

b   4, 5.73 and 229.57

Answer:

_____

## QUESTION 9                                     2 marks

Subtract the following.

a   196 from 813

Answer:

_____

b   5556 from 9223

Answer:

_____

## QUESTION 10                                    2 marks

Use division to solve:

a   $4824 \div 3$

Answer:

_____

b   $84.2 \div 0.4$

Answer:

_____

## QUESTION 11                                    4 marks

Using BODMAS, solve:

a   $(3 \times 7) \times 4 + 9 - 5$

Answer:

_____

b   $(8 \times 12) \times 2 + 8 - 4$

Answer:

_____

# Section C: Trade Mathematics

## Basic operations

### Addition

QUESTION 1                                              1 mark

An electrician uses 8 m, 22 m, 17 m and 53 m of different types of conduit over 2 months. How much conduit has been used in total?

Answer:

_____

QUESTION 2                                              1 mark

An electrician charges $227 for labour and $498 for parts. How much is the total bill?

Answer:

_____

### Subtraction

QUESTION 1                                              1 mark

A work van is filled up with 36 L of LPG. The tank is now at its maximum of 52 L. A driver uses the following amounts of LPG on each day:

Monday: 5 L

Tuesday: 11 L

Wednesday: 10 L

Thursday: 8 L

Friday: 7 L

How many litres of LPG are left in the tank?

Answer:

_____

QUESTION 2                                              1 mark

If an electrician has 224 capacitors in stock and 179 are used over 2 months, how many are left?

Answer:

_____

## Multiplication

QUESTION 1                                              1 mark

An electrician uses 2 multifunction time relays, 4 resistors and 7 capacitors on one job. How many multifunction time relays, resistors and capacitors would be used on 12 similar jobs?

Answer:

_____

_____

QUESTION 2                                              1 mark

To connect different electrical parts on the one job, the following wires are used: 2 m of green wire, 3 m of red wire and 1 m of yellow wire. How much of each wire would be used doing the wiring on 15 similar jobs?

Answer:

_____

_____

## Division

QUESTION 1                                              2 marks

An electrician has a box of 250 resistors.

a  How many jobs can be completed if each standard job requires 6 resistors?

Answer:

_____

b  Will any be left over?

Answer:

_____

QUESTION 2                                              1 mark

If an apprentice electrician earns $288.80 for working a 5-day week, how much is earned per day?

Answer:

_____

# Decimals

## Addition

### QUESTION 1                                          1 mark

An electrician's tool belt and a hole-saw set are purchased for $17.99 and $56.50 respectively. How much will be paid in total?

Answer:

_____

### QUESTION 2                                          1 mark

An electrician buys a multimeter for $18.75, electrical tape for $6.95, a headlight bulb for $4.95 and a crimping set for $17.50. How much has been spent in total?

Answer:

_____

## Subtraction

### QUESTION 1                                          1 mark

An electrician has a 4 L can of de-greaser. It is used on three different electrical cleaning jobs: 1185 mL for job 1, 1560 mL for job 2 and 1135 mL for job 3. How much is left?

Answer:

_____

### QUESTION 2                                          1 mark

An electrician has a 35 m reel of aerial cable. If 15.48 m is used on one job, 12.76 m is used on another and 3.44 m is used on the last job, how much is left on the reel?

Answer:

_____

## Multiplication

### QUESTION 1                                          1 mark

An apprentice replaces 6 fluorescent light bulbs at a cost of $6.99 each and 4 light switches at a cost of $11.99 each. What is the total amount spent?

Answer:

_____

### QUESTION 2                                          1 mark

A packet of 100 single screw electrical connectors costs $38.50. If an electrician uses 6 packets, how much is the total cost?

Answer:

_____

## Division

### QUESTION 1                                          1 mark

An electrician takes 12 hours to complete 3 small jobs around a house. His total bill amounts to $582.48. How much does he earn per hour?

Answer:

_____

### QUESTION 2                                          1 mark

A workshop owner buys 240 electrical connectors in bulk at a total cost of $3600. How much is the cost of one electrical connector?

Answer:

_____

## Fractions

### QUESTION 1                                          1 mark

$\frac{2}{3} + \frac{3}{4} =$

Answer:

_____

### QUESTION 2                                          1 mark

$\frac{4}{5} - \frac{1}{3} =$

Answer:

_____

### QUESTION 3                                          1 mark

$\frac{2}{3} \times \frac{1}{4} =$

Answer:

_____

## QUESTION 4                                1 mark

$$\frac{3}{4} \div \frac{1}{2} =$$

Answer:

_____

# Percentages

### QUESTION 1                                2 marks

An electrical repair bill comes to $2546.00.

a   How much is 10% of the bill?

Answer:

_____

b   What is the final bill once the 10% is taken off?

Answer:

_____

### QUESTION 2                                2 marks

An apprentice buys an electrician's manual on DVD and an electrical wood metal stud detector. The total comes to $37.80.

a   How much is 10% of the bill?

Answer:

_____

b   What is the final bill once the 10% is taken off?

Answer:

_____

# Voltage, current and resistance

## Voltage

### QUESTION 1                                1 mark

What is the voltage in a circuit that has a current of 5 A and a resistance of 10 Ω?

Answer:

_____

### QUESTION 2                                1 mark

What is the voltage in a circuit that has a current of 15 A and a resistance of 16 Ω?

Answer:

_____

# Current

### QUESTION 1                                1 mark

What is the current in a circuit with a voltage of 6 V and a resistance of 3 Ω?

Answer:

_____

### QUESTION 2                                1 mark

What is the current in a circuit with a voltage of 240 V and a resistance of 6 Ω?

Answer:

_____

# Resistance

### QUESTION 1                                1 mark

What is the resistance of a circuit with a voltage of 12 V and a current of 2 A?

Answer:

_____

### QUESTION 2                                1 mark

What is the resistance of a circuit with a voltage of 240 V and a current of 12 A?

Answer:

_____

# Measurement conversions

## QUESTION 1                                1 mark

How many millimetres are there in 3.85 m?

Answer:

_____

## QUESTION 2                                1 mark

How many metres does 2285 mm convert into?

Answer:

_____

# Measurement — length and area

## Circumference

### QUESTION 1                               2 marks

Find the circumference of a warehouse light fitting with a diameter of 80 cm.

Answer:

_____

### QUESTION 2                               2 marks

Find the circumference of a pulley with a diameter of 15 cm.

Answer:

_____

## Area

### QUESTION 1                               2 marks

An electrical workshop measures 45 m by 12 m. What is the total area?

Answer:

_____

## QUESTION 2                                2 marks

A light switch cover is 11.5 cm by 10.5 cm. What is the total area?

Answer:

_____

# Earning wages

## QUESTION 1                                2 marks

A first-year electrical apprentice earns $280.60 net (take home) per week. How much does she earn per year? (Note that there are 52 weeks in a year.)

Answer:

_____

## QUESTION 2                                2 marks

A car has major electrical damage after a fire. The labour bill comes to $2860. If the auto-electrician spends 70 hours working on the car, what is the rate for labour per hour?

Answer:

_____

# Squaring numbers

## QUESTION 1                                2 marks

What is $9^2$?

Answer:

_____

## QUESTION 2                                2 marks

A workshop has an area for a hoist that is $8.2 \times 8.2$ m. What is the total area?

Answer:

_____

# Ratios

## QUESTION 1                                    2 marks

A driver cog has 20 teeth and the driven cog has 60 teeth. What is the ratio, in the lowest form, of the driver cog to the driven cog?

Answer:

_____

## QUESTION 2                                    2 marks

The ratio of the diameters of driver pulley A to driven pulley B is 1 : 4. If the diameter of driver pulley A is 15 cm, what is the diameter of driven pulley B?

Answer:

_____

# Mechanical reasoning

## QUESTION 1                                    1 mark

Pully 1 and pully 2 each measure 5 cm across their diameters. Pully 3 measures 10 cm across the diameter. How many times will pulleys 1 and 2 turn if pully 3 turns 3 times?

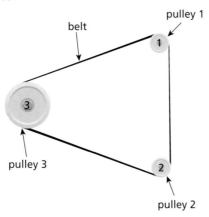

_____

## QUESTION 2                                    1 mark

Each cog in the below diagram has 16 teeth and they interlock with one another. If cog 5 turns in an anticlockwise direction, which way will cog 1 turn?

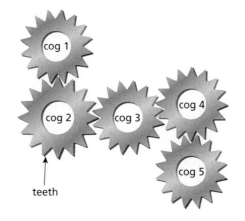

_____

# Glossary

**Alternating current (AC)**   An electric current that reverses direction at regular recurring intervals

**Ampere (amp)**   A unit of electric current

**Bus bar**   A heavy copper bar used as the primary power source to carry heavy currents. A bus bar can also be used to make a common connection between several circuits

**Capacitor**   An electrical device that consists of two conducting surfaces that are oppositely charged and that are separated by a thin layer of insulation material

**Circuit**   A system of conducting parts through which an electrical current flows

**Circuit-breaker**   A device that automatically opens a circuit should the current exceed the rated amount. The circuit-breaker can also be re-set

**Conduit**   A pipe or tube through which electrical wires or cables can be transferred

**Current (I)**   The transfer of electric charge through a conductor. It is measured in amperes

**Cycle**   A complete positive and a complete negative alternation of voltage or current

**Direct current (DC)**   An electric current in which there is a non-stop transfer of charge in one direction

**Farad**   The unit of measurement for capacitance

**Frequency**   The number of complete cycles in a unit of time. The unit of measurement for frequency is hertz

**Fuse**   An electrical device of wire or a strip of fusible metal that can melt and therefore open a circuit if the current exceeds the rated amount. A safety device that destroys itself and is replaced with a new fuse

**Horsepower**   A unit of power equal to 746 W of electrical power

**Insulator**   A material that has high resistance to the flow of an electric current

**Joule**   A unit of electrical energy

**Junction box**   A box for inserting and joining cables or wires

**Kilowatt (kW)**   A unit of electrical power equal to 1000 W

**Kirchoff's law**   The sum of the currents entering a junction is equal to the sum of the currents leaving that junction

**Ohm**   A unit of measurement for resistance

**Ohm's law**   Current is directly proportional to voltage and inversely proportional to resistance

**Parallel circuit**   A method of connecting a circuit so that the current has two or more paths to follow

**Power**   The rate of doing work. The unit for power is watts

**Resistance (R)**   The opposition a material gives to the flow of electrons. It is measured in ohms

**Volt (V)**   A unit of electrical potential or pressure

**Voltage**   The electromotive force or electrical pressure that is measured in volts

**Voltage drop**   The potential difference measured across current-limiting elements in a circuit

**Watt (W)**   A unit of measure of power

**Wavelength**   The distance travelled by a wave during the time interval covered by a cycle

# Formulae and data

## Circumference of a Circle

$C = \pi \times d$

where: $C$ = circumference, $\pi$ = 3.14, $d$ = diameter

## Diameter of a Circle

Diameter ($d$) of a circle $= \dfrac{\text{circumference}}{\pi(3.14)}$

## Area

Area = length $\times$ breadth and is given in square units

Area $= l \times b$

## Voltage

Voltage ($V$) = current ($I$) $\times$ resistance ($R$)

$$V = I \times R$$

## Current

Current ($I$) $= \dfrac{\text{voltage } (V)}{\text{resistance } (R)}$

$$I = \dfrac{V}{R}$$

## Resistance

Resistance ($R$) $= \dfrac{\text{voltage } (V)}{\text{current } (I)}$

$$R = \dfrac{V}{I}$$

# Times Tables

**1**

| | | | |
|---|---|---|---|
| 1 × 1 | = | 1 |
| 2 × 1 | = | 2 |
| 3 × 1 | = | 3 |
| 4 × 1 | = | 4 |
| 5 × 1 | = | 5 |
| 6 × 1 | = | 6 |
| 7 × 1 | = | 7 |
| 8 × 1 | = | 8 |
| 9 × 1 | = | 9 |
| 10 × 1 | = | 10 |
| 11 × 1 | = | 11 |
| 12 × 1 | = | 12 |

**2**

| | | |
|---|---|---|
| 1 × 2 | = | 2 |
| 2 × 2 | = | 4 |
| 3 × 2 | = | 6 |
| 4 × 2 | = | 8 |
| 5 × 2 | = | 10 |
| 6 × 2 | = | 12 |
| 7 × 2 | = | 14 |
| 8 × 2 | = | 16 |
| 9 × 2 | = | 18 |
| 10 × 2 | = | 20 |
| 11 × 2 | = | 22 |
| 12 × 2 | = | 24 |

**3**

| | | |
|---|---|---|
| 1 × 3 | = | 3 |
| 2 × 3 | = | 6 |
| 3 × 3 | = | 9 |
| 4 × 3 | = | 12 |
| 5 × 3 | = | 15 |
| 6 × 3 | = | 18 |
| 7 × 3 | = | 21 |
| 8 × 3 | = | 24 |
| 9 × 3 | = | 27 |
| 10 × 3 | = | 30 |
| 11 × 3 | = | 33 |
| 12 × 3 | = | 36 |

**4**

| | | |
|---|---|---|
| 1 × 4 | = | 4 |
| 2 × 4 | = | 8 |
| 3 × 4 | = | 12 |
| 4 × 4 | = | 16 |
| 5 × 4 | = | 20 |
| 6 × 4 | = | 24 |
| 7 × 4 | = | 28 |
| 8 × 4 | = | 32 |
| 9 × 4 | = | 36 |
| 10 × 4 | = | 40 |
| 11 × 4 | = | 44 |
| 12 × 4 | = | 48 |

**5**

| | | |
|---|---|---|
| 1 × 5 | = | 5 |
| 2 × 5 | = | 10 |
| 3 × 5 | = | 15 |
| 4 × 5 | = | 20 |
| 5 × 5 | = | 25 |
| 6 × 5 | = | 30 |
| 7 × 5 | = | 35 |
| 8 × 5 | = | 40 |
| 9 × 5 | = | 45 |
| 10 × 5 | = | 50 |
| 11 × 5 | = | 55 |
| 12 × 5 | = | 60 |

**6**

| | | |
|---|---|---|
| 1 × 6 | = | 6 |
| 2 × 6 | = | 12 |
| 3 × 6 | = | 18 |
| 4 × 6 | = | 24 |
| 5 × 6 | = | 30 |
| 6 × 6 | = | 36 |
| 7 × 6 | = | 42 |
| 8 × 6 | = | 48 |
| 9 × 6 | = | 54 |
| 10 × 6 | = | 60 |
| 11 × 6 | = | 66 |
| 12 × 6 | = | 72 |

**7**

| | | |
|---|---|---|
| 1 × 7 | = | 7 |
| 2 × 7 | = | 14 |
| 3 × 7 | = | 21 |
| 4 × 7 | = | 28 |
| 5 × 7 | = | 35 |
| 6 × 7 | = | 42 |
| 7 × 7 | = | 49 |
| 8 × 7 | = | 56 |
| 9 × 7 | = | 63 |
| 10 × 7 | = | 70 |
| 11 × 7 | = | 77 |
| 12 × 7 | = | 84 |

**8**

| | | |
|---|---|---|
| 1 × 8 | = | 8 |
| 2 × 8 | = | 16 |
| 3 × 8 | = | 24 |
| 4 × 8 | = | 32 |
| 5 × 8 | = | 40 |
| 6 × 8 | = | 48 |
| 7 × 8 | = | 56 |
| 8 × 8 | = | 64 |
| 9 × 8 | = | 72 |
| 10 × 8 | = | 80 |
| 11 × 8 | = | 88 |
| 12 × 8 | = | 96 |

**9**

| | | |
|---|---|---|
| 1 × 9 | = | 9 |
| 2 × 9 | = | 18 |
| 3 × 9 | = | 27 |
| 4 × 9 | = | 36 |
| 5 × 9 | = | 45 |
| 6 × 9 | = | 54 |
| 7 × 9 | = | 63 |
| 8 × 9 | = | 72 |
| 9 × 9 | = | 81 |
| 10 × 9 | = | 90 |
| 11 × 9 | = | 99 |
| 12 × 9 | = | 108 |

**10**

| | | |
|---|---|---|
| 1 × 10 | = | 10 |
| 2 × 10 | = | 20 |
| 3 × 10 | = | 30 |
| 4 × 10 | = | 40 |
| 5 × 10 | = | 50 |
| 6 × 10 | = | 60 |
| 7 × 10 | = | 70 |
| 8 × 10 | = | 80 |
| 9 × 10 | = | 90 |
| 10 × 10 | = | 100 |
| 11 × 10 | = | 110 |
| 12 × 10 | = | 120 |

**11**

| | | |
|---|---|---|
| 1 × 11 | = | 11 |
| 2 × 11 | = | 22 |
| 3 × 11 | = | 33 |
| 4 × 11 | = | 44 |
| 5 × 11 | = | 55 |
| 6 × 11 | = | 66 |
| 7 × 11 | = | 77 |
| 8 × 11 | = | 88 |
| 9 × 11 | = | 99 |
| 10 × 11 | = | 110 |
| 11 × 11 | = | 121 |
| 12 × 11 | = | 132 |

**12**

| | | |
|---|---|---|
| 1 × 12 | = | 12 |
| 2 × 12 | = | 24 |
| 3 × 12 | = | 36 |
| 4 × 12 | = | 48 |
| 5 × 12 | = | 60 |
| 6 × 12 | = | 72 |
| 7 × 12 | = | 84 |
| 8 × 12 | = | 96 |
| 9 × 12 | = | 108 |
| 10 × 12 | = | 120 |
| 11 × 12 | = | 132 |
| 12 × 12 | = | 144 |

9780170464031

# Multiplication Grid

|     | 1  | 2  | 3  | 4  | 5  | 6  | 7  | 8  | 9   | 10  | 11  | 12  |
| --- | -- | -- | -- | -- | -- | -- | -- | -- | --- | --- | --- | --- |
| 1   | 1  | 2  | 3  | 4  | 5  | 6  | 7  | 8  | 9   | 10  | 11  | 12  |
| 2   | 2  | 4  | 6  | 8  | 10 | 12 | 14 | 16 | 18  | 20  | 22  | 24  |
| 3   | 3  | 6  | 9  | 12 | 15 | 18 | 21 | 24 | 27  | 30  | 33  | 36  |
| 4   | 4  | 8  | 12 | 16 | 20 | 24 | 28 | 32 | 36  | 40  | 44  | 48  |
| 5   | 5  | 10 | 15 | 20 | 25 | 30 | 35 | 40 | 45  | 50  | 55  | 60  |
| 6   | 6  | 12 | 18 | 24 | 30 | 36 | 42 | 48 | 54  | 60  | 66  | 72  |
| 7   | 7  | 14 | 21 | 28 | 35 | 42 | 49 | 56 | 63  | 70  | 77  | 84  |
| 8   | 8  | 16 | 24 | 32 | 40 | 48 | 56 | 64 | 72  | 80  | 88  | 96  |
| 9   | 9  | 18 | 27 | 36 | 45 | 54 | 63 | 72 | 81  | 90  | 99  | 108 |
| 10  | 10 | 20 | 30 | 40 | 50 | 60 | 70 | 80 | 90  | 100 | 110 | 120 |
| 11  | 11 | 22 | 33 | 44 | 55 | 66 | 77 | 88 | 99  | 110 | 121 | 132 |
| 12  | 12 | 24 | 36 | 48 | 60 | 72 | 84 | 96 | 108 | 120 | 132 | 144 |

# Notes